BLAZERS®

LINE OF DUTY

THE U.S. SECRET SERVICE
PROTECTING OUR LEADERS

by Connie Colwell Miller

Reading Consultant
Barbara J. Fox
Reading Specialist
North Carolina State University

Content Consultant
Kenneth E. deGraffenreid
Professor of Intelligence Studies
Institute of World Politics
Washington, D.C.

Capstone
press®

Mankato, Minnesota

Blazers are published by Capstone Press,
151 Good Counsel Drive, P.O. Box 669, Mankato, Minnesota 56002.
www.capstonepress.com

Library of Congress Cataloging-in-Publication Data
Miller, Connie Colwell, 1976–
    The U.S. Secret Service: protecting our leaders/by Connie
Colwell Miller.
    p. cm. — (Blazers. Line of duty)
    Summary: "Describes the Secret Service, including what it is and what
Secret Service agents do" — Provided by publisher.
    Includes bibliographical references and index.
    ISBN-13: 978-1-4296-1275-3 (hardcover)
    ISBN-10: 1-4296-1275-4 (hardcover)
    1. United States. Secret Service — Juvenile literature. 2. Secret service —
United States — Juvenile literature. I. Title. II. Series.
HV8144.S43M55 2008
363.28'30973 — dc22   2007024828

Editorial Credits
Jennifer Besel, editor; Bobbi J. Wyss, designer; Wanda Winch, photo researcher

Photo Credits
AP Images/Akron Beacon Journal/Ken Love, 25; Marty Lederhandler, 12; Reed
    Saxon, 6; U.S. Secret Service, 24
Corbis/Reuters/Jorge Silva, 13; Kevin LaMarque, 8–9
Getty Images Inc./AFP/Brendan Smialowski, 4–5; AFP/Mandel Ngan, 17, 28;
    AFP/Nicholas Kamm, 10–11; AFP/Paul J. Richards, cover, 21, 22–23;
    AFP/Tim Sloan, 15, 29; Mark Wilson, 19, 26–27; Matthew Cavanaugh, 14
Zuma Press/The Sacramento Bee/Anne Chadwick Williams, 18

1 2 3 4 5 6 13 12 11 10 09 08

TABLE OF CONTENTS

STOPPING CRIMINALS

A man gets ready to shoot the president. But the **criminal** is caught before he can act on his plans.

[**criminal** — someone who commits a crime]

6

A **hacker** tries to steal money from a bank. Instead, he is arrested and put in jail.

[**hacker** — a person who breaks into computer systems]

7

Secret Service agents stop criminals. Agents move quickly to keep our leaders and our money safe.

 The Secret Service calls a person they are protecting a "protectee."

SECRET SERVICE BASICS

The Secret Service is a law enforcement **agency**. Agents guard U.S. leaders and their families. They follow the leaders day and night.

[**agency** — a government office that provides a service]

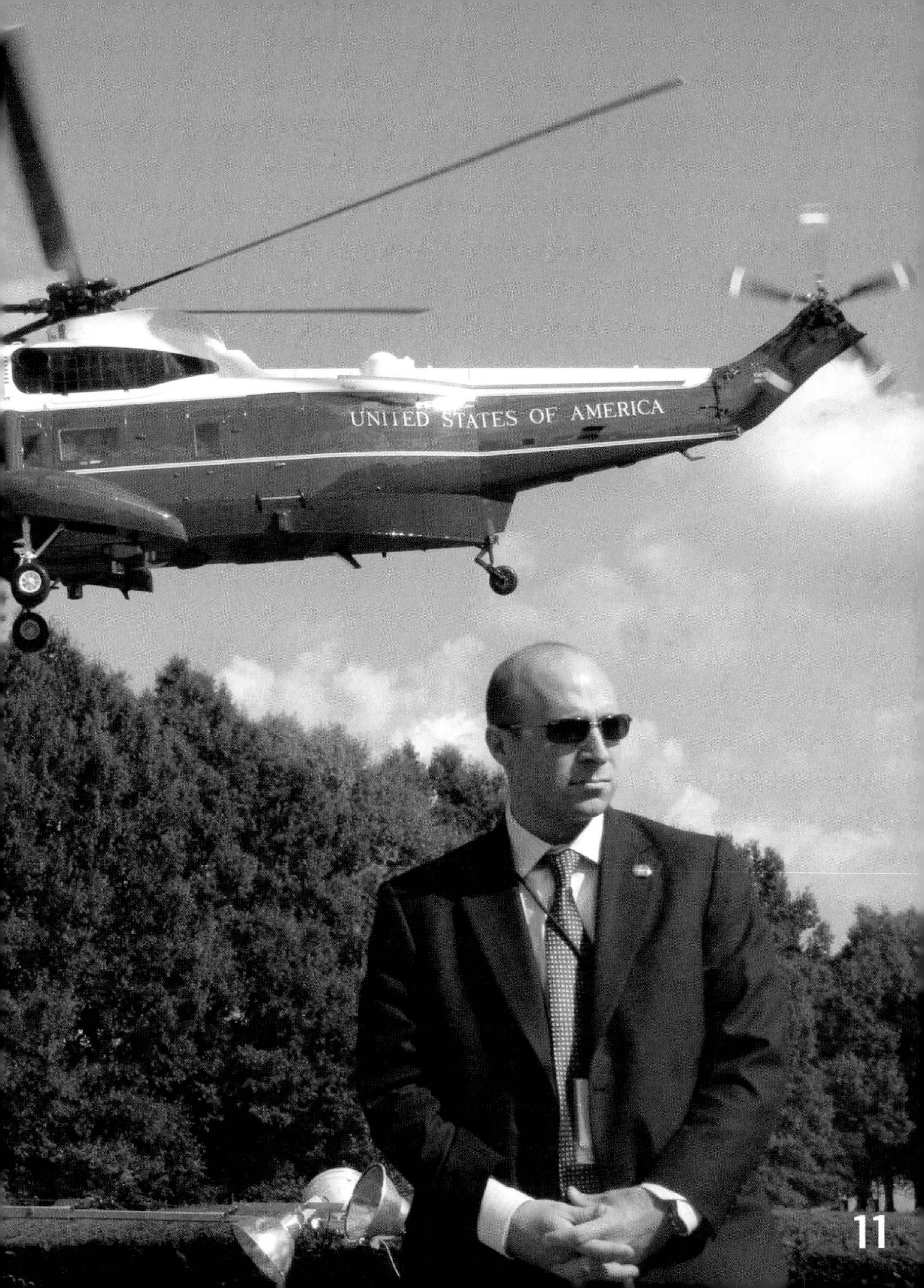
UNITED STATES OF AMERICA

The Secret Service watches over other people as well. Former presidents are guarded by the service. Visiting world leaders are protected too.

former Palestinian leader Yasser Arafat

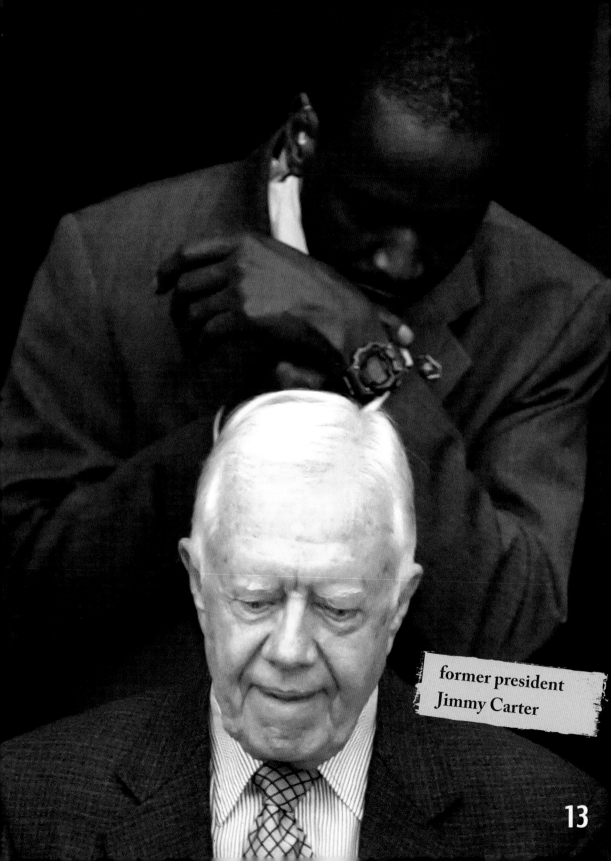

former president
Jimmy Carter

13

When a leader travels, so does
the Secret Service. Agents make
sure the route is safe. They block
roads to control who comes and goes.

FACT! New agents go through 27 weeks of training.

STREET CLO
TO ALL PEDESTRI

STOP

ALL
VEHICLES
SUBJECT
TO SEARCH

AREA
AHEAD

NO

Agents stay with U.S. leaders even in other countries. Agents watch for people who might try to hurt or kill the leaders.

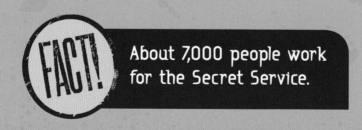

About 7,000 people work for the Secret Service.

Agents guard the U.S. Secretary of State and the White House Chief of Staff in foreign countries.

The Secret Service also stops crimes that deal with money. Agents hunt down people who make fake money.

Agents guard the U.S. Treasury Building. People working there manage the country's money.

 The Secret Service was formed in 1865 to stop people from making fake money.

WEAPONS AND EQUIPMENT

Secret Service agents carry guns and handcuffs. They wear bulletproof vests. They also carry a radio to keep in touch with other agents.

Some agents use trained dogs. These dogs sniff out bombs. They lead agents to the weapons before they **explode**.

[**explode** — to blow up]

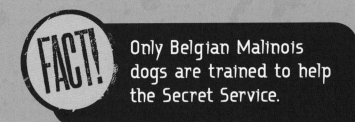

FACT! Only Belgian Malinois dogs are trained to help the Secret Service.

Agents use computers to track criminals. Many criminals steal money using the Internet. Agents find these people and arrest them.

Secret Service agents often work with
U.S. Marshals to arrest criminals.

IN THE LINE OF DUTY

Agents are often in the line of fire. Some criminals try to shoot U. S. leaders. Agents have to be ready to do anything to keep our leaders safe.

FACT! The guards on the roof of the White House are part of the Secret Service. They protect the building and the people in it.

Secret Service agents risk their lives every day. The agents are ready for any trouble that comes their way.

GLOSSARY

agency (AY-juhn-see) — a government office that provides a service to the country

arrest (uh-REST) — to capture and hold someone for breaking the law

criminal (KRIM-uh-nuhl) — someone who commits a crime

explode (ek-SPLODE) — to blow apart

hacker (HAK-ur) — a person who is an expert at getting into a computer system illegally

route (ROUT) — the road or course followed to get somewhere

READ MORE

Beyer, Mark. *Secret Service.* Top Secret. New York: Children's Press, 2003.

Seidman, David. *Secret Service Agents: Life Protecting the President.* Extreme Careers. New York: Rosen, 2003.

INTERNET SITES

FactHound offers a safe, fun way to find Internet sites related to this book. All of the sites on FactHound have been researched by our staff.

Here's how:
1. Visit *www.facthound.com*
2. Choose your grade level.
3. Type in this special code **1429612754** for age-appropriate sites. You may also browse subjects by clicking on letters, or by clicking on pictures and words.
4. Click on the **Fetch It** button.

FactHound will fetch the best sites for you!

INDEX